Limestone Diary

Poetry from a decade in a twin soul's transformation
2004-2014

Shahana Dattagupta

a Flying Chickadee publication

ISBN-13: 978-0-9896263-9-2 (*Limestone Diary*)
ISBN-10: 0-9896263-9-3

First printing: March, 2015
Flying Chickadee
www.flyingchickadee.com

All original art on cover and in interior ©2015 by Shahana Dattagupta

for

Muralidhar

03.27.15

"He's more myself than I am. Whatever our souls are made of, his and mine are the same."
– Emily Bronte

"I am in you and you in me, mutual in divine love."
– William Blake

"He had been told by his parents and grandparents that he must fall in love and really know a person before becoming committed. But maybe people who felt that way had never learned the universal language. Because, when you know that language, it's easy to understand that someone in the world awaits you, whether it's in the middle of the desert or in some great city. And when two such people encounter each other, and their eyes meet, the past and the future become unimportant. There is only that moment, and the incredible certainty that everything under the sun has been written by one hand only. It is the hand that evokes love, and creates a twin soul for every person in the world. Without such love, one's dreams would have no meaning.
Maktub…"
– Paulo Coelho, *The Alchemist*

*****

"Whether you succeed or not is irrelevant… making your unknown known is the important thing."
– Georgia O'Keeffe

∞

CONTENTS

A NOTE ON TWIN SOULS   1

PART I   2004-2006

Soul In The Mirror   7
Blue Iris   9
A Thought For Tomorrow   11
Blue And Yellow, Pink And Brown   13
Sands In My Palms   15
Some Of My Things   16
Lament Of The Lot   19
Limestone Diary   21
Retraction To Womb   23
Faith   25

PART II   2011-2014

Again And Again   29
Surrender   31
I-And-Thou   32
Like Water To Earth   35
Solitude   36
Let Me   38
Rang-e-Khuda   40
For Every Kind Of Mother   42
Childhood's Gate   47
To The Holy Music Of Unity   49
This Uni-verse   51

PART III   Today

A Day Like Any Other   55

GRATITUDE   57

A NOTE ON TWIN SOULS

From my very infancy, I had a poignant knowing of having separated from Oneness, the greater whole of Love, which many call by many names. Intrinsic to that knowing was also the constantly felt presence of a "soul half," with whom I was joined in pure, true Love. Between ages 2 and 7, I was intensely aware of having parted from someone all-important, with a related purpose around true Love in the world. I felt a big-eyed wonder and a pressing feeling in my chest that often threatened to burst forth as tears. Goethe's grand poem *The Holy Longing* reflects my soul's calling well.

By my late teens, allowing myself to be conditioned by rationalist culture and education that focus on an objective reality, I lost my innate compass to the ways of "real" life. Almost. As if preprogrammed by Nature, in the Spring of 2004, a few months shy of my 30th birthday, I spontaneously awoke to the twin soul connection and at once also to the greater Oneness. My life was redirected to a calling I couldn't yet name. By October that year I spontaneously coined the term "twin soul" without having heard of such a thing anywhere, and today it is used by many to describe much of what I have experienced all my life!

My initial awakening was reflected in someone who served as a catalyst for a fuller remembrance of unconditional Love, and its inextricably linked creative, healing and spiritual expression in service. Over the next 7 years my entire life was turned upside down, and every single aspect of its existence and expression became radically transformed by the power and understanding of (divine) Love.

Then, through the year 2011, while working on my memoir of essays, *Thrive! Falling in Love with Life,* I began experiencing intense intuitive and mystical premonitions about "the return of the twin soul incarnate," which inexplicably heightened at the full moon. In October, in the midst of my book's release, I experienced a vivid "visitation" with my world-renowned, esteemed Guru of music, during which I confessed to having "Krishna in my heart."

Miraculously, within 7 days I stood facing a beautiful soul from several longitudes away, not only born on a full moon but also synchronously connected with me since my very birth – across timelines and geographies – just as I had sensed all along! Words fail to convey the soaring joy of recognition, unspoken and profound understanding, spacious peace, and pure Love and Oneness – all instantly known. Along with an implicit, shared commitment to humbling soul growth, greater purpose, and service simply through presence. *This* was the felt presence I had known all my life! Thereafter I experienced another 3 years of what I humorously call my "cosmic education via quantum entanglement."

Whether my experience is random or meaningful, myth or truth, illusion or reality, you'll have to know for yourself. What I can offer is that for more than a decade I've been compelled deep, deep into the rabbit hole of expanding consciousness. Through a progressive dissolution of "the self" into complete soul unity with "the other" and thereby into Oneness, I receive endless, wordless "downloads" of claircognizant knowing. And I am schooled with realizations in the nature of creation, consciousness and Love, that transform the very fiber of my being. As the inner knowing fully embodies, it is as if accumulated ancestral impressions from all time are being released from my cellular memory to reverse the concept of division, for a return home to Oneness. With unity consciousness comes a reversal to childlike innocence and play, an experience of the Mother-Father-Guru-God within One-Self, and also the innate knowing of the integration and harmonizing of the yin and yang energies, sacred sexuality, soul marriage... All that can heal, *from within*, the illusory worldly paradigm of division and separation, which externally manifests as inequity, patriarchy, racism, homophobia, violence, war, disease and environmental imbalance. Because the soul's relationship to its exact and opposite reflection – experienced as the divinely beloved "other"– is the microcosm of Oneness, it is the "unit" of transformation of consciousness, and is thereby of profound, direct service to the world.

What I have awakened to through *this* education makes me what I am (not) today. It keeps me at once exalted and humbled, and it gifts me extraordinary creative, healing and spiritual abilities, which enable me to serve in a humble yet singular way. Most importantly, it radically transforms how *I am* in this world of duality and separation, as it shows me every day that (however lost or heinous in appearance), there is no "other," only The One. And so, there is not much more to *do* but to *be* ... in Oneness.

The 22 poems in this book came through me in the two book-ends of the decade-long, rabbit hole experience. I offer them as a sacred gift to my twin soul and to all of you. If the essential message of Oneness is all you take away, this gift will have served its purpose.

And in the rare and precious event that you too experience the sacred gift (and responsibility) of the twin soul connection, I wish you, first and foremost, a great sense of humor and play! You will most enjoy this miraculous course in true Love that grows you into your highest Self and enables you to serve with your singular Gift, when you see that this is cosmic play, a meaningful and significant quantum entanglement meant to make us go "Aha!" and "Ha Ha!" all the way! The title of Dante Alighiery's allegory, *The Divine Comedy*, is a wonderful allusion to the knowing that spiritual awakening is really an endeavor of light, wit, playfulness, silliness and good humor.

And for all the times you may feel painfully lost, afraid, sad or confused (because the outer world doesn't yet match what you know within), I wish you endless courage, patience, gratitude, fortitude, humility, surrender and faith, so you may stay gently and firmly on your pathless path of Love, awakening, transformation and humble, daily, *embodied* enlightenment. Wait, did I mention humor and play?

As the great Lao Tzu said in his collection of paradoxes (koans) in the Tao Te Ching, one of the wisest books ever written: *The path into the light seems dark, the path forward seems to go back, the direct path seems long ... the greatest wisdom seems childish ... the greatest love seems indifferent.* May you rest lightly and sweetly in the unerring knowing that all paths, however apparently lost, pointless or divergent, always return home... to Love.

And really, *we are already always there.*

In Love,
Shahana
February 18, 2015

∞

PART I

2004-2006

This section reveals the arc from my initial remembrance of the twin soul connection (and thereby a connection to my own higher Self and Oneness), to a sharp fall back into separation consciousness and the related period of intense inner burnishing (often termed a "Dark Night of the Soul"), and finally, a surrender to faith and Love.

Soul In The Mirror

Oh, Soul in the Mirror,
You do make me see:
What I really used to be;
What I may never again be.

For every word, a word,
For every glance, a glance,
For every touch, a touch,
And for every sigh, a sigh –

I see my hopes, dreams
But mostly my ideals
Magnified in reflection:
Sharpened into focus.

Trapped and chained in
A cage of my own making;
Comfort and complacency
Stifle me to delirious ending.

Oh, Soul in the Mirror,
Why did you make me see:
What I really used to be;
What I may never again be?

∞

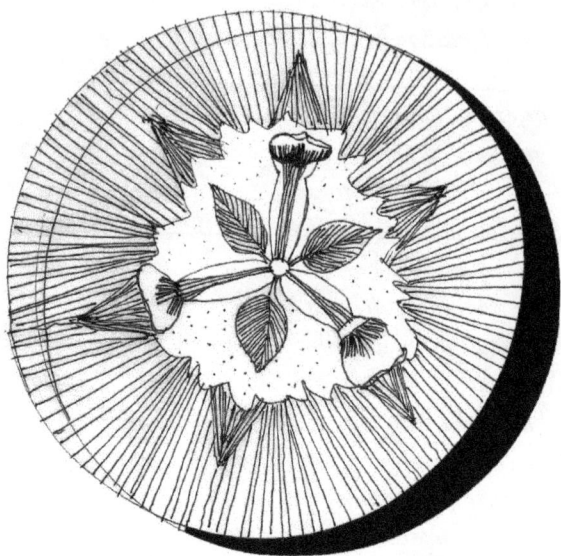

Blue Iris

(Yet) Another wondrous idea strikes,
And the Blue Iris further deepens,
Then widens, melts and outpours –
Like the limitless expanse of sea!

Far, far in the horizon
The lofty dream, (a hope), shimmers
Undaunted by the setting flame –
Forever anticipating tomorrow's sunrise!

Endless, indefatigable (in) spirit,
Boundless, unfettered (in) mind,
Pristine, generous (in) heart –
This childlike, bottomless blue wonder!

Oh Blue Iris, never wither,
Oh Blue Iris, never fade,
Oh Blue Iris, forever bloom,
Oh Blue Iris, forever dream!

∞

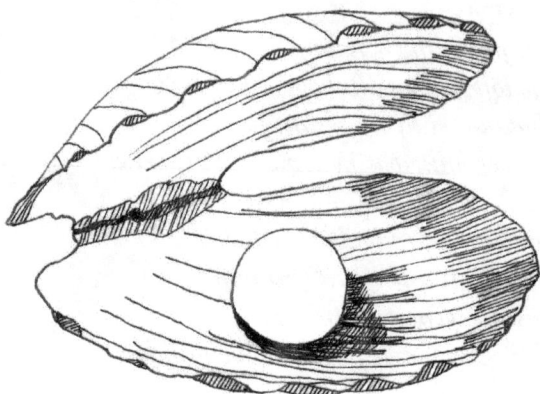

A Thought For Tomorrow

A furrowed brow, a pregnant pause, a sigh:
A shadow fleetingly paints the countenance.
He wishes to convey the nebulous to her
But retreats into the mazelike mind:
To secret passages and clever hideouts.
Steeped in a thought-feeling palimpsest,
Hours later when the moment has passed,
A distilled kernel emerges; he tells himself:
Tomorrow I will gift her with this pearl!

Oh, but Tomorrow is another day —
With its unique form, music and color;
There are new rays of sunshine;
There is a budding scent in the air;
Fledgling green on canopies of trees
Adorned with fresh droplets of dew;
Much newness to ponder, to race toward!
The moment relents to another Tomorrow:
Oh, she already knows; she must know.

∞

Blue And Yellow, Pink And Brown

A haunting baby scent
Of freshly bathed skin;
A fine, silken nest
Forms a mop of sunshine;
Layers of golden yellow
And snatches of blue;
A lobe-edge she traces
To a mysterious dimple,
And long slender fingers
Tell her endless tales.

Robust fleshy forms
As if unexplored terrain,
And a detailed essay
In black, pink and brown;
Flowing dark tresses
Envelope as the night;
A mouth that, he says,
Is a well-kept secret,
And eyes that, he says,
Never cease to smile.

Full-spectrum color,
Music and rhythm;
Timeless hours of glory,
Streaming tears of Heaven;
Intertwining of tendrils,
Playing of heartstrings;
A union of twinsouls,
A meeting of heartminds;
A swirling mix of hues:
Blue and yellow, pink and brown.

∞

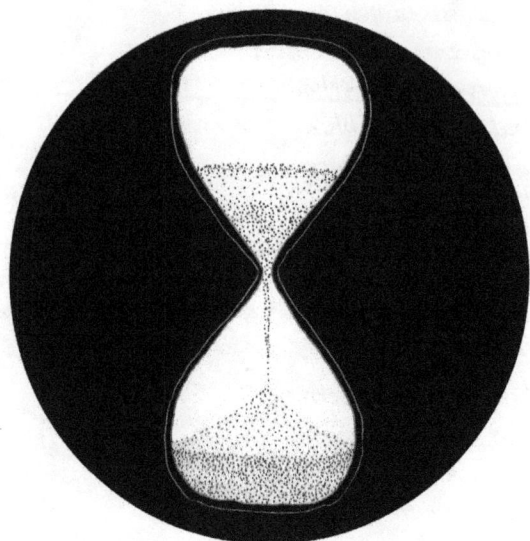

Sands In My Palms

Sands in my trembling palms,
Cupped gently and lovingly;
Textures fine and comforting,
Colors glistening, shimmering.

A delicate hold one needs
To fight time and gravity;
A stifling grasp may find
Hopeless, merciless slithering.

Sands of time, sands of love,
Ever poignant, tender a scene:
A test of strength and courage,
Of selfless, unconditional loving.

Stand still and freeze, oh time,
That I may nourish and cherish
This moment of eternal bliss:
Sands in my palms, mesmerizing.

∞

Some Of My Things

A purple-and-gold saree,
A soft white cotton petticoat
And a deep maroon bindiya,
In a bag, you easily returned.
But you have with you, my jaan,
My many priceless things!

With you is every instance
That I knew your subtle mind,
That I felt your implicit need,
That I lavished love unabashed.
With you is every ray of light
That I painted into your dreams!

In your floor must surely seep
The patter of my prancing feet.
By your chair must quietly mull,
A sketch of my remotest thoughts.
And at your beside must lie
A bundle of my deep reveries.

With you are my melodies,
My ideas, secrets and dreams,
Each glance of tenderness,
And the love in every morsel.
With you are my laughter bells,
And my priceless pearly tears...

In your air must surely resound
Loud chimes of my optimism.
In your water must bubble and flow
My spirit and my exuberance.
In your mirror must glimmer
The purest reflection of my soul.

You have with you, my jaan
Every flame of our passion,
And every dance of our bodies.
You have with you, my jaan,
The magic sparkle in my eyes,
And every smile I left behind.

∞

* Inspired by the poetry of Gulzar in the song *Mera Kuchh Samaan* in the film
Ijaazat, 1987

Lament Of The Lot

I was but an errant corner,
And I was a curious shape.
Wrapped in messy tangles,
Treads across my chest,
I was a lotus in the swamp!
I was the implausible sketch:
One on which to not build.

She suitably fits the mold,
She does make worldly sense.
A square, regulated visage,
A legitimate societal place,
Among winners she resides!
You've drawn elaborate plans:
Plans on which to build.

Indebted you are for her,
I am yours unfettered!
Yet circumstance prevails:
Build on her you truly must,
While I must ruefully sell.
Tested, tried ground is she:
I remain, unborn, an ideal.

∞

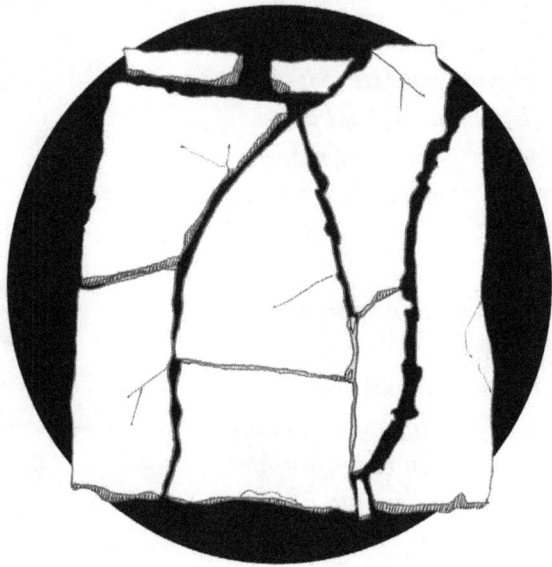

Limestone Diary

Sandwiched layers of many a time,
A palimpsest formed in pallid lime.

Peeling flakes in memory lane,
Sharply etched hieroglyphs of pain.

Screaming and deafening voices
Waft in and out of consciousness:

What a mistake! Mother had cried,
Wipe that pearl! Father had vied.

You're my puppy love, one had said;
You're dispensable, he later said.

You're my best friend, another had said;
You are a horrid bitch, he later said.

You're nutty and lovely, one had said;
You don't interest me, he later said.

You're the Goddess, another had said;
You are but a whore, he later said.

You deserve the world, one had said;
You deserve a beating, he later said.

I'll be who you want, I had said.
I shall be only who I am, I later said.

You're my twinsoul, I sensed he said;
You're not the one, he later said.

∞

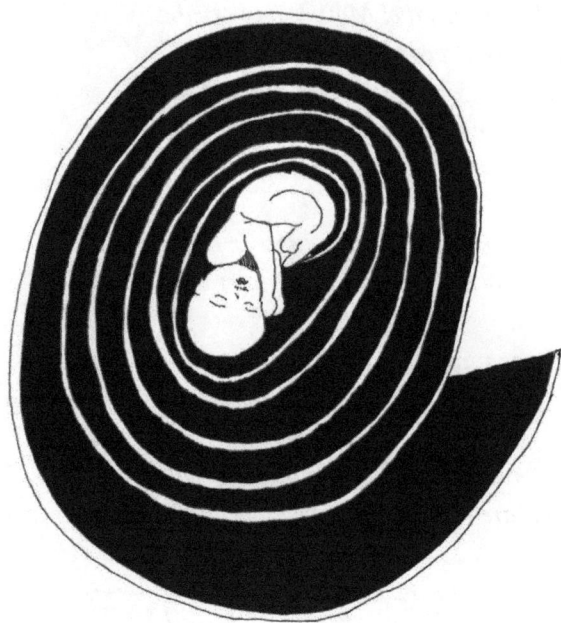

Retraction To Womb

Ragged edges, towering Tetons,
Washes of a silver lunar bloom.
How the very same instance:
As red canyons were witnessed
Awakening to a flaming solar flush.

Mutation of a curving lamppost:
A torana fleetingly; no, a dragon.
Thrown amidst ancient Kowloon,
Roaming, seeking, wide-eyed,
Drenched in clouds of incense.

A drizzle on foreign Pacific lands,
Yes, distant Western civilization.
But hungry nostrils inhale to head
Intoxicating sweet scents:
Maiden monsoons soothing earth.

Eyes closed, ears to chugging;
A goods train by Seattle's waterfront.
Reverberations in the child's heart,
Tumbling on, to thriving Calcutta:
A humid summer with grandparents.

Drapes of precise machined quilting,
Drifts of somnolence, dreams;
Chequered patterns press on flesh,
Embraces of retired, soft cottons:
Love-sewn, baby kantha-blankets.

Tight curl of body, as a kidney bean,
Welling cravings for swirling pools,
Cocooning blackness, the envelope:
That time just after conception, but
Just before memory ever known.

∞

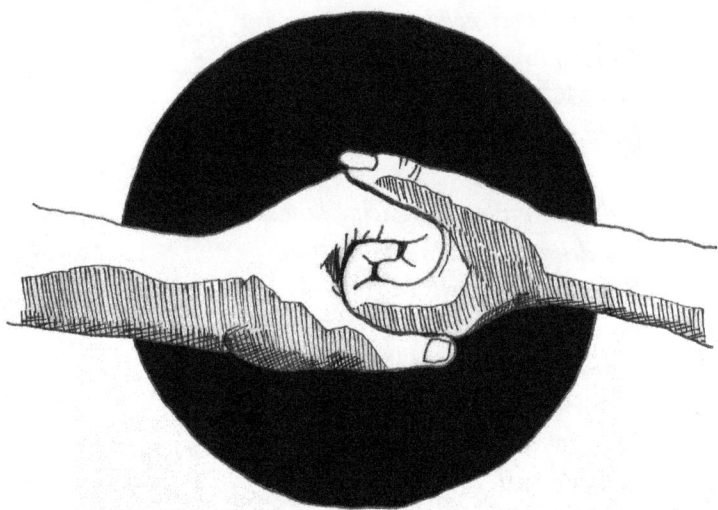

Faith

A breeze skims, whispering
Pithy little mantras, offerings;
Laughing waves kiss ashore
Promising patterns, hope galore;
Bids goodbye an orange glory,
Reassuring but a morning story.

At the outset weak, faltering,
Then with surer, firmer footing,
First an infant of maiden tread;
Then a toddler, brisk instead.
Now, then! I break into a run,
Curious child in wild abandon.

Flights of inexplicable faith,
Quests of ever elusive truth;
Afar the horizon my gaze finds,
Still, a palm extends behind –
For a deep faith does stand
That reach out will your hand.

At Your behest, oh my Lord
I question not, only applaud;
Prance I do toward eternity:
For as do parallel lines at infinity,
I with the One who does create
And twinsouls shall forever unite.

∞

PART II

2011-2014

This section of poetry unfolded after my complete and unconditional surrender to twin soul consciousness, and eventually, a progressively embodying awakening in divine Love. It reveals how, through the divinely gifted beloved, one experiences Mother-Father-Guru-God within One-Self, a complete reversal to childlike innocence in Oneness, and ultimately, the sacred marriage of souls within One-Self.

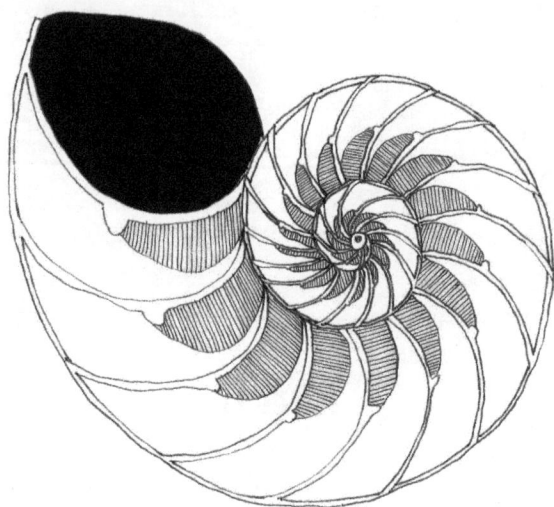

Again And Again

I love you
With every pore of my being,
In every moment and every breath,
Again and again.

I love you
Enough to forget my little self,
And to let you go...
Again and again.

I love you
Enough to remember my Higher Self,
And to stay on Divine purpose...
Again and again.

∞

Surrender

Molten-brown sees pure-blue,
My gaze searches for You,
You, who has stolen everything,
Left me stripped, with nothing:
Naked, transparent, vulnerable,
A raw pinkness unbearable,
With heart cracked open,
And soul bared, drunken.

Yet from such sheer nakedness,
This utter defenselessness,
From this fragile pink flower
Rises authentic, ultimate power;
For she who has surrendered,
Let all be seen and plundered,
Has nothing more to fear,
And no mask to hold dear.

So unleash riches; in submission,
Even in humbling prostration,
From the abundant Life-Force,
The Limitless, the very Source;
And like to sea the river gushing,
Or to flame the moth rushing,
Radiant Love can't help but glow:
Into Your silence it must flow.

∞

I-And-Thou

I recall that momentous moment:
The twinsoul in recognition,
That eerie, uncanny knowing, and
All known before in annihilation.

At first I caught in your eyes
A fleeting glimmer of my soul;
Then the image blossomed into
My very purpose and my role.

Long and hard I reached for you
Knowing that we are one;
We're meant to walk together
That path toward The One.

He who brought us face-to-face
Had yet a grander design:
First make purer your heart, He said,
Relinquish all longing but Mine!

So, off I marched into the world
To do or die of higher calling;
Everywhere I sought to follow
Unconditional Love's bidding.

Losing self in creative action —
In giving, living and loving;
Burnished by the fire of Love
I felt radiant purity emerging.

*Humbled by His immense power
To transform me inside-out,
I let deepening Love make me
Both the lover and the devout.*

*Now, in this sacred resonance
I hear His urging to become still:
Return to Me your purpose, your doing,
Even your errors, and your will!*

*In allowing Him to mold me thus,
To sculpt me down to my core;
I find no longer me, nor you,
And not even Him anymore!*

*In here there is left no quest —
Nothing to learn, nor know,
Nothing but the boundless Love
That merges all in I-and-Thou.*

∞

*Title resonant with Martin Buber's work *Ich und Du*, and poetic expression
with Kabir *Bani*. Later also discovered a resonance with *Not-Two Is Peace* by
Adi Da Samraj, and the Persian couplet by Amir Khusro incorporated by Ustad
Amir Khan into his *tarana* in Raag Hamsadhvani:
*Etihaade-st miyaan e man o tu
Man o tu neist miyaan e man o tu*
Translates to:
*There's a union between You and I
(Such that) there's no "You" and "I" between You and I*

Like Water To Earth

Bathed pure in loving reverence,
When the dark clouds were gone,
When the sun was shining
And the mountain was out,
And I'd befriended the moon;
When I was looking deep within
Or far, far into the skies,
Sure of no more wonder to behold –
Then, it came: the miracle of you.

You, who came unannounced,
Subtly, quietly, unnoticed,
Seeping into my consciousness
You soaked up my soul,
Like water to earth –
Washing away the last wounds,
Filling my pores with gentleness,
Enveloping me in liquid embrace,
Drenching me in fluid warmth.

And so I am replenished, returned
To my softest, pliant, richness
With sweet-smelling petrichor,
Fragrant, fertile, verdant, lush;
Like water to earth –
You've made deep wellsprings
That will bubble up and rise,
And then – the water will break
For the next burst of Creation.

∞

Solitude

I thought I was alone
In my reverie
Then what's that I hear you say?

Oh wait that's the slow
Whoosh-whoosh of breath
Filling me with the force of Life
Through which I can feel
The atmospheric layers shifting
And cosmic storms brewing
Now there's that soft
Dhuk-dhuk of my heart
Beating louder as I tune in
Moving me with the rhythms of Life
Through which I can hear
The Big Bang and Shiva's dance
In an ongoing moment of Creation
And Re-creation
Then suddenly there's a warm
Throb-throb here and another there
The hot gushing of blood
Of energy
Carrying me with the flows of Life
Through which I can see how
You my friend in Pakistan and I
Are undeniably instantly eternally
Connected
As sisters
Oh and how you my friend
Across the continent and I
Are undeniably instantly eternally
Connected
As twin souls
And cosmic lovers

Then as I grow stiller
The whispers beats and flows cease
The hard edges of mind-body blur
I see hear smell taste feel nothing
And bask instead
In a warm glow of Light
The blissful oneness with You

In this being but no-being
I now hear tiny tiny whispers
And see vivid spectacular visions
Pieces of the puzzle rapidly
Snapping into place
And in that fleeting moment
The entire Universe is revealed
And Life's deepest sacred secrets are
Made utterly simple –
Truth

Truth
That in the instant uttered
Will be made false
Through the limitations of
Word Time Space Ego
Of the smallness of human telling
And listening
So brushing off the temptation for
Blurting sharing teaching
I kneel to the ground
Palms folded to my heart
Or spread open and upward
I lean into the stillness
And sit with the inner knowing
Graced by the company of You
In solitude

∞

Let Me

Let me dive headlong
into this magnificent ocean
Let me float not
but immerse fully
in its torrential waters
Let me wash away
the duality of you and me
Let me know only
the profound waters
that engulf false separateness
Let me be swept away
into the bottomless depths
Let me flail my arms
and even cry in desperation
Let me be threatened
in loss of breath and life
Let me drown so far
as to hit rock bottom
And let me die...

Let me then be born again
in those still calm blue waters
where all illusions
of loss absence and death
are forever relinquished

Let me open my eyes to
the miraculous life of Truth
that thrives at the oceanbed
of true Love
And let me experience how
in such utter surrender
in unquestioning faith
in unerring knowing
this Love that all callously doubt
magically breathes new life
into my eternal being
Let me then rise as a phoenix
and soar high
in the intense joy
of this sweet homecoming

Let me delight in knowing again
what I already know
Let me
Love
You
Let me
Be

∞

* Resonant with the Urdu couplet by Amir Khusro:
Khusro dariya prem ka, ulti va ki dhaar:
Jo utra so doob gaya, jo dooba so paar
Translates to:
Khusro says, the river of love flows in paradox:
S/he who skims it is fated to drown,
And s/he who immerses makes it home

Rang-e-Khuda

My fingers strain stretch spread
To touch You who is invisible
Instead they uncode patterns
And hidden messages in
The flutter of butterfly wings
The swaying of wheat grasses
The rhythm of the woodpecker

Through the envelope of darkness
I stretch my hand farther high
To reach toward the heavens
Perhaps to catch a sunbeam
A measure of Your Light
Instead I am sprinkled by
The drip of morning dew
The mist of the foaming spring
The spray of crashing waves

I grope the earth to find You
Instead my fingers stumble upon
A lost forlorn squeaking chick
Buried under rustling leaves
Prey to the foraging stray cat
My hearing locates mama's cries
To reunite her with her newborn
Just as surely as I can always return
To the sound of granny's tender call

In my unending unerring quest
For You who has kept me from sight
But has generously given me vision
I see with my mind's eye
With the windows of my heart
That You exist nowhere —but
In the long blades of grass
In the beak of the baby bird
In the texture of stripped wood
In the sounds of the woodpecker
In the soft wrinkles of granny's hand
In the contours of sister's face
And in the eternal hapless wait
For father's unreachable Love

For only when my heart so breaks
Can all walls finally crumble
And reveal the secret door
To that chamber deep within
Where You've been hiding all along
You to whom I've been blind
You whom seeing eyes cannot see
And feeling fingers cannot touch
Except in the being of true Love
Which once known can glow
From inside out — shining Light
So all darkness can forever go
And I can finally see You
Because I can finally see me

∞

* Inspired by the film of the same name *(The Color of Paradise,* 1999) by Majid
Majidi

For Every Kind Of Mother

First there's the mother
Who channels me into light,
Who knows my fingers and toes
And my hungry little cries;
She knows my heartbeat
Without my ever saying why.
She holds me by the hand
As I walk tentative steps,
She watches over me
As I grow even in my sleep,
And she pleads for my wellness
As I burn with a fever.
I pray to Shiv-Shakti, she says
For you to be in our lives.
She uncovers every talent,
As I form into expression,
And she applauds with pride
As I find my unique stride.
For this kind of mother
I say my deepest gratitude,
The labors of whose womb
Birth me into full bloom.

Then there's the mother
Who shows me a new life,
Who learns all about me
And my little idiosyncrasies;
She knows my heart's choice
Without my ever saying why.
She holds me subtly close
As I locate my place,
She respects my ways
As I indeed respect hers,
And she slowly opens her heart
As I fully offer mine.
I pray to Ganesha, she says
For your lifelong togetherness.
She beholds but, aghast
As I clutch shattered dreams
And then she sets me free
As I beg to part ways.
For this kind of mother
I say my deepest gratitude,
The labors of whose prayers
Birth me to unknown waters.

And then there's the mother
Who in a time of darkness,
Takes me as her own:
Had I a daughter, she'd be just like you.
She knows my heartbreak
Without my ever saying why.
She holds me to her chest
As I learn to breathe again,
She makes that phone call
As I wander around lost,
And she cooks up a roast
As I hanker for comfort.
I pray to Jesus, she says
For you to find your way.
She eggs me on to break free
As I struggle with the past,
And she points the way
As I wonder what's to come.
For this kind of mother
I say my deepest gratitude,
The labors of whose heart
Birth me to a new start.

Now there's the mother
Who radiates the Light,
Who knows my true purpose
And my soul's higher calling;
She knows my heart's nature
Without my ever saying why.
She holds me by intention
As I fly higher and higher,
She reminds me of me
As I shed the false layers,
And she tells me all is possible
As I harbor fleeting doubt.
I pray to Saraswati, she says
For you to be fully you.
She emanates quiet blessings
As I evolve in consciousness,
And she witnesses in silence
As I find my greatest joy.
For this kind of mother
I say my deepest gratitude,
The labors of whose soul
Birth me into complete whole.

For every kind of mother
I say my deepest gratitude;
For how blessed am I
To have not one but a few!
Yet I know them not apart
For, each could be the other –
Joined as Mother Goddess,
As One Soul of Motherhood.
For all these beautiful souls,
I say my deepest gratitude;
The labors of whose Love
Birth me daily and anew.

∞

Childhood's Gate

With you I walked through Childhood's Gate
Me racing ahead and you a tad bit late
Promising to create side by side
A universe of love and sweetness and light

With you I walked through Childhood's Gate
Then fell from Grace to witness hate
But your whispers hugged me in eternal faith
So I kept going in sunshine and shade

With you I walked through Childhood's Gate
Releasing all memory for a fully clean slate
Revealing a canvas as blank as can be
To paint fresh creations of all possibility

With you I walked through Childhood's Gate
A stroll in the garden with my twinsoul mate
A moment of pause at the ancient tree
Welcoming the little girl to return to me

With you I walked through Childhood's Gate
Sharing little bites from the very same plate
Singing together melodies of no-time
Of harmony and homecoming for all-time

With you I walked through Childhood's Gate
Alchemized pure to the virginal state
Returned to the innocence of not-knowing
And the wordless silence of all-knowing

With you I walked through Childhood's Gate
To know there is nothing but a timeless spate
No birth no death only a marriage of souls
For the ongoing moment of Creation whole

∞

To The Holy Music Of Unity *(An Ode To The Guru)*

An ancient poem speaks, you see,
Of two lovely birds in a tree:
One (a Guru) that is thee
And one (a chela) that is me.

At first you are Master
And I am ardent follower,
Only in your Light's shower
Can I, the tender bud, flower.

I bloom, I shed, I fall apart,
In your witness I birth my art,
You watch and simply play your part
While 'I' must die to open my heart.

In many rounds of death and birth
I finally see in bright-eyed mirth,
Your finger steady, pointing to Truth:
To the light within, to limitless fruit.

In surrender I see how I and thee,
We both live inside of me:
One we are in divinity,
The two birds are the same, you see!

I salute thee, my Guru, eternally –
Who watches for hours endlessly,
Lovingly, patiently, relentlessly,
Forever and unconditionally…

So I may know to forget me,
To lose the illusion of duality;
And awaken to the One in Me,
To the holy Music of Unity.

∞

This Uni-verse

That I am the eternal
And I am everywhere
You need no word with me
Only know I am always (t)here

As you explore green lands
And take flight in blue skies
Every flower and ray of light
Is I before your eyes!

Each time beauty stirs your soul
And your eyes fill with tears
You'll know: She whispers to me
Or: She somehow always hears...

I am (in) your heart and soul
I am (in) every breath
I am (in) your dreams and actions
I am (in) your faith

And so writes itself a poem
For which there is no end
You-and-me is this Uni-verse
On earth a fleeting godsend

∞

PART III

Today

This poem is my daily gratitude for having been divinely gifted my twin soul at birth, making every day a re-birth-day!

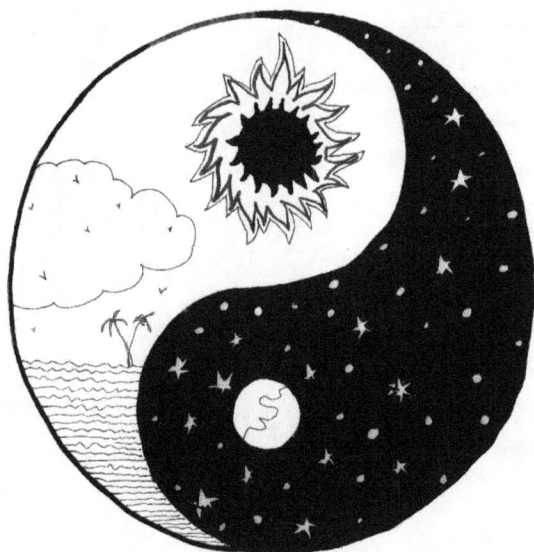

A Day Like Any Other

A day like any other, for
Destined it is to roll on by;
'Tis naught to all 'n sundry,
But priceless to loving eye.

A day like any other, and
Nothing but moon run wild,
Save for gentle begetting
Of a Krishna-like golden child.

A day like any other, but...
The full moon, an electric night
Tell of an Appalachian fest:
A twin soul's here; a twin's in sight!

A day like none other –
This day a forever celebrity,
The day two mirrors brought together
To reflect and know full humanity.

A day like none other –
This day to joyfully greet;
A day that if had not been,
Yin with Yang never complete.

A day like none other –
This day to eternally remain
A day that if had not been,
A twin soul's quest in vain.

∞

GRATITUDE

To my beloved twin soul;

To all souls – seen and unseen – who have birthed, catalyzed, guided, witnessed, blessed and loved the twin souls;

To all souls who transform themselves through twin soul / unity consciousness and service in divine Love;

To all souls who are energy healers, lightworkers, starseeds and indigo messengers during this powerful time of ascension of human consciousness;

Special heartfelt thanks to Jenna Forrest for channeling, healing, teaching and guiding about sensitive souls and twin souls (www. profoundhealingforsensitives.com). Finding Jenna's soulful work in October 2011 greatly illuminated, encouraged and inspired my pathless path. Thanks also to: Paulo Coelho of Brazil for his beautiful allegorical explorations of the Twin Soul / Soul Mate's connection with one's Personal Legend / Gift (*The Alchemist*, 1988; *Brida*, 1990); Charles Eisenstein (previously professor at Penn State University), for his prolific writing and speaking on the ascension of human consciousness (including soul relationships), and the connection with a vast number of planetary topics (http://charleseisenstein.net); Anthon St Maarten of South Africa for his work on divine destiny (www. anthonstmaarten.com). Synchronistically connecting with the works of these three individuals in early 2015, while working on this sacred book, served my faith in birthing it into the world.

∞

Other books by Shahana Dattagupta

Ten Avatars
A collection of stories
Flying Chickadee, March 2010

Thrive! Falling in Love with Life
Flying Chickadee, November 2011

You Are Michelangelo, and You Are David!
Awakening the Creative and Creation Within
Flying Chickadee, March 2013

Chickadee and the Cat
A different kind of love story
Flying Chickadee, March 2014

∞

www.ingramcontent.com/pod-product-compliance
Lightning Source LLC
Chambersburg PA
CBHW020512100426
42813CB00030B/3209/J